CW00556096

TYNE AND WEAR
FIRE & RESCUE

An Illustrated History

DAVE WALMSLEY

FIREKAT

Warehouse Blaze – Newcastle Quayside, December 1989

FOREWORD
CHIEF FIRE OFFICER IAIN BATHGATE

Tyne and Wear fire and Rescue Service came into existence in 1974 and, at the time of writing, has provided its services to the people of Tyne and Wear for over 35 years.

As with all organisations the service has undergone considerable change over this period of time, both in terms of improved equipment and training as well as in conditions of service and working practices.

What has not changed however, is the ongoing commitment of the staff to the work that we do and their desire to provide the best possible service to the people we protect. That commitment and belief was evident to me when I first joined the service in July 1978 and is still equally evident today.

This book captures, pictorially, this abiding spirit and I hope you will enjoy reading it and viewing the journey of Tyne and Wear Fire and Rescue Service from 1974 to the present. I also trust that, for many, the book will bring back proud memories and will also be a source of information for those who did not serve but who have an interest in work of the fire and rescue service.

Iain Bathgate
Chief fire Officer
Tyne and Wear Fire and Rescue Service

To all the personnel of
Tyne and Wear Fire & Rescue Service
Past and present

First published 2009

FireKat Ltd
PO Box 1250
Sunderland
Tyne & Wear
SR5 9FD

www.twfire.com

Copyright © Dave Walmsley, 2009

Published by FireKat Ltd.

The right of Dave Walmsley to be identified as the Author
of this work has been asserted in accordance with the
Copyrights, Designs and Patents Act 1988.

All rights reserved. No part of this book may be reprinted
or reproduced or utilised in any form or by any electronic,
mechanical or other means, now known or hereafter invented,
including photocopying and recording, or any information
storage or retrieval system, without the permission in writing
from the Publishers.

British Library Cataloguing in Publication Data.
A catalogue record for this book is available from the British Library.

ISBN 978-0-9563871-0-3

Typesetting and origination by FireKat Ltd.   www.firekat.co.uk

Printed in Great Britain.

Contents

Introduction

It could be said that the formation of Tyne & Wear Metropolitan Fire Brigade, (that later became Fire & Rescue) was very much a case of 'Hobson's Choice'. The new Tyne & Wear Brigade amalgamated every fire station, with its men, appliances and equipment, falling within its boundary line. This was drawn under the Local Government Re-organisation Act of 1974, creating the Metropolitan County.

That line was not drawn with the convenience of local fire brigades in mind. Therefore major problems came from three factors. 1. Stations now just inside the boundary had lost most of their previous station area. 2. Resources coming from six different brigades differed considerably as did procedures & standards. 3. Combined numbers of personnel, transferring in from the original brigades, were not sufficient to meet the establishment needs of the new brigade.

The naming of the County after its two major rivers was very appropriate. For each of the seven constituent authorities, (Newcastle, Gateshead, Sunderland, South Shields, Tynemouth, parts of Durham & Northumberland) bordered upon at least one of the rivers at some point.

At approximately 208 square miles it was one of the most compact of the new brigades. At the time shipbuilding yards and engineering industries filled the urban areas, alongside two city centres, an airport, motorways and a mix of industrial estates and rural areas. Populated by over 1.2 million residents, it presented a very comprehensive and concentrated fire and life-risk area to be protected.

The job of successfully integrating this mix of personnel and equipment from six different brigades, into a cohesive firefighting force, fell to the new Chief Fire Officer, Pat Watters.

At 00.01 hours on 1st April 1974 the Brigade was 'born' almost entire in its concept. The nationally agreed decrease of working hours, from 56 to a 48 hour week was to be implemented in November of that year. Therefore recruitment was required on a large scale to staff appliances. A large influx of new firemen started in this year – a 17% increase in the size of the workforce. This was achieved without lowering standards. In fact, in the recruiting drive, a statistic was utilised using the phrase, "Are *You* the 'One in Ten' We're Looking For?" (only one in ten applicants achieved the required standard).

The standard of fire appliances did vary. From AECs to ERFs, Commers & Bedfords, to Dodge. Not all met with the CFO's approval. To improve this it was decided that Dennis would be the machine of choice for standardisation throughout the brigade. This started with the F109 and progressed through the F131 & RS/SS series. Volvo became the vehicle of choice in the 80's before reverting to the Dennis Sabre in later years, with a final mix of the two.

Fire stations likewise were of variable quality and age but progressively building stock was improved. With PFI (Private Finance Initiative) the ability to standardise stations was enabled. The true community aspect of the service could also become a reality.

Through community fire safety initiatives and legislative reforms prevention became a focus as well as emergency response.

A new control centre at Pilgrim Street became the mobilising system for the whole brigade. Centralising all incoming emergency calls and turnouts through VF(A). (Voice Frequency system A).

1977 saw the first national firemen's strike lasting 9 weeks, during which Armed Forces personnel answered emergency calls, with ageing Green Goddesses. The result was a rise and a pay formula that was to last over 25 years.

January 1979 saw a further reduction in hours to 42, requiring the introduction of a new Watch – Green. This was added to the existing Red, White and Blue.

Innovations such as the 'cab reader' were just the start of a steady progressive improvement in appliances, equipment, clothing and protection, over the following years.

This book shows snapshots, through the decades, of the history of Tyne & Wear Fire & Rescue Service. In 2009 it is in its 35th year of operation. From 1974 it has protected and served the citizens of Tyne & Wear with dedication and professionalism. Long may it continue to do so. We look forward with interest to the next thirty-five years.

Acknowledgements

I would like to thank the following organisations and individuals for their assistance with this project. Without their contributions and permissions the undertaking would not have been possible.

Chief Fire Officer Iain Bathgate and his predecessor CFO Richard Bull. Brigade Photographer, the late Joe Nevison, Newcastle Chronicle & Journal, The Sunderland Echo, Sunderland Library & Local Studies, Fire Magazine, Newcastle Library & Local Studies, Tyne & Wear Museums & Archives, Durham & Darlington Fire & Rescue Service.
John Adamson, John Allsopp, the late Dennis Barker, Graeme Bowser, Joe Clapperton, Dave Clark, Phil Davison, Derek Dunwoodie, Alex Fairgrieve, Jeff Foster, Dave Garrett, Trevor Geddes, Ron Henderson, Alan Holmes, Bob Hope, Arthur Lockyear, Paul Mathews, Colin McDonald, Mark McMullen, Mick Nielsen, Sam Nicholson, Dave Royal, Alex Ryles, Russ Seth, Gordon Smith, Stuart Thompson, Kieth Trotter, Martin Woods, Gary Yates.

It is to the photographers, both professional and amateur, that I would like to convey my grateful thanks. Without them being in the right place, at the right time, none of the excellent photographs in this book would be available for us to enjoy.
Long may their shutters, digital or otherwise, continue to snap, at the fleeting moments of Fire Service history as it passes us by.

Also to the personnel of the Tyne & Wear Fire & Rescue Service, who *are* the organisation, doing what they do, day in day out, 24/7.

ONE

In The Beginning

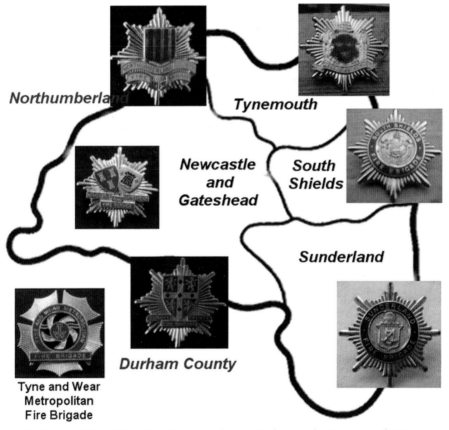

Northumberland

Tynemouth

Newcastle
and
Gateshead

South
Shields

Sunderland

Durham County

Tyne and Wear
Metropolitan
Fire Brigade

Badges of the Brigades that amalgamated into the Tyne and Wear
Metropolitan Fire Brigade

Above: **Dennis Fire Appliance F109.** St Mary's Lighthouse. Soon to be the standard pumping appliance throughout the brigade. A diesel engine with automatic gearbox and rear mounted pump. Roof monitor & high pressure hose reels. 'Backwards' fire sign lit up.

Opposite Top: The new Tyne and Wear Metropolitan Fire **Brigade Headquarters** were located at Pilgrim Street, Newcastle. Previously Newcastle & Gateshead Fire Service HQ. An ERF pump and Turntable Ladder (still in N&G colours) bask in the sun on the forecourt. A police car (Vauxhall Victor) exits from the tunnel adjacent Police HQ.

Below: **TL Reversing.** DELTA 03 blocks the whole of Pilgrim Street.

Bottom: **Brigade First Day Cover.** Sent to all personnel on formation. The stork flies over the new Brigade badge, historic fire engines are illustrated on the stamps. 'T over W' original badge. 1st April 1974.

Bottom Left: **Pat Watters** became the first Chief Fire Officer of Tyne & Wear on its formation on 1ˢᵗ April 1974. He was previously the CFO of Newcastle & Gateshead Fire Service from 1967. He was thus familiar with the region and ideally placed to forge the amalgamation of the county brigades into the new metropolitan. Later became a HMI.

Bottom Right: **'Flames Across the Tyne'** was a book on the history of the Newcastle & Gateshead Fire Service. It was written by Gerry March with the design and illustrations by Ross Hickling. Published in 1974, just before the amalgamation, it is long out of print and quite collectable. 'New' HP (Hydraulic Platform) on the front cover.

Opposite Bottom Right: **Tools of the Trade.** The type 'A' branchpipe. Top type is a diffuser model, made of solid brass for durability they were very heavy. A nozzle spanner was required to change the jet size.

P. Watters Q.F.S.M. F.I.Fire E.
Chief Fire Officer 1974 - 1978

FLAMES ACROSS THE TYNE

Above: **The Callers Fire** of November 1969, featured in the N&GFS history book. Christmas decorations can be seen across the street as firefighters battle with jets. £2m worth of damage was caused and 15 pumps, 88 firefighters and 20 water jets were used over five hours to contain the blaze. L/Fm Harry Louvre received a Queens Commendation for his actions.

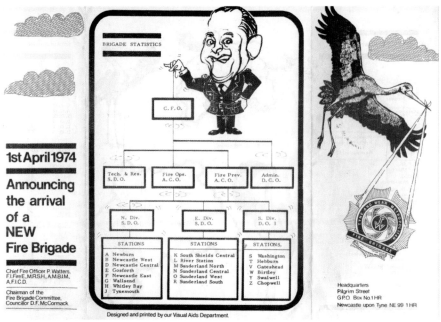

Above: **Brigade Birthday Card.** Sent to all personnel on amalgamation. Separatism is replaced by togetherness. Pat Watters pulls the strings. Printed by the newly formed 'visual aids' department.

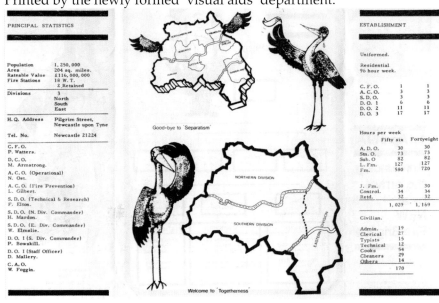

Above: **AEC 305VTN.** West End, Newcastle, .Derek Dunwoodie & Stew Bell beside an old Newcastle & Gateshead Appliance. Original colours were maroon and red. It has a mid-ships mounted pump.

Above Right: **Newcastle & Gateshead Fire Tunic Button**

Above: **Mess Room.** Stn BRAVO, West End, Newcastle. 1970's. Raised TL can be seen in drill yard through left hand side window.

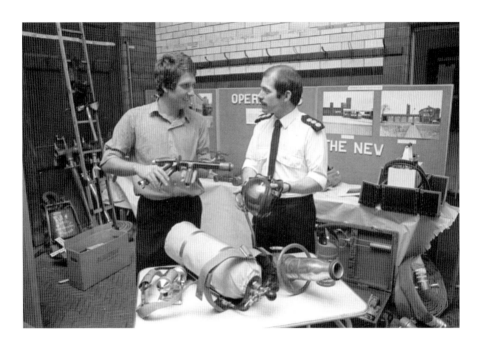

Above: **New Equipment.** A display of new equipment is shown here by Bill Edminson and Alan Holmes. They hold the new hosereel gun and Draeger BA (Breathing Apparatus) set. On the left can be seen old kit-hook ladder, ball type standpipe and foam knapsack tank. New 5X foam branch and BCF (halon) extinguisher are on the table, 'New' station Romeo (Tunstall) is in photo behind. Alan wears ADO rank markings-defunct for some years- recently revived as "Station Manager". Early 70's Station NOVEMBER, Sunderland Central.

Below: **Volleyball.**To keep fit, Stn FOXTROT, Fossway, Newcastle, 1974

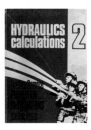

16

Above: **Control Room.** Stn DELTA, Pilgrim St., Newcastle, 1974
At the rear can be seen the appliance deployment board. The three
divisions divided by blue lines.

Above: **Doreen Dabrowsky**, takes an emergency call at control.

Above: **Fire Boat.** Stn 'LIMA' -soon defunct, South Shields, river station.
Opposite Below Right: **Recruiting Leaflet**, 1974 style.
Below Left: **Kit Check** at Stn DELTA, Newcastle, with hats.
Below Right: **Brigade Badges.** The subtle change that came later. The 'T over W' becomes 'W over T'. Still unique, with gold 'fishtails' instead of silver star shape commonly used.

Above and Below: **Leading from the Front.** Men of action: SDOs show how it's done, H. Mardon (Ndiv) top, Bill Elmslie (Ediv) bottom.

Above: **Dodge 50′ HP Airborne.** Washington, November 1975.
Sunderland Airport -'airborne' Derek Dunwoodie does a driving test for engineers to demonstrate instability of design. Previously a sand tipper wagon, it ended up with a lead filled front bumper and lower tyre pressures. It then became known as the 'lead sled'.

Above: **Draeger DSU**   *Above:* **Car Opener**   *Above:* **Zip Gun**

Above: **Ritchie's Garage.** Hetton-Le-Hole, Romeo & Oscar White Watch

'**WHIRLPOOL**' was the first magazine of the new Tyne & Wear Brigade. Picture shows Charlie Collier (left) in front of sailors who assisted at a sisal warehouse fire at Corporation Quay, Sunderland. Autumn, 1974.

Above: **Rear** of the main hall.

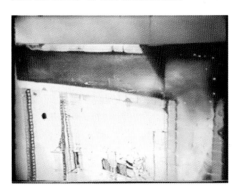

Above: **Usworth Comprehensive School.** Washington, November 1974. A severe fire which practically destroyed the school, its main block and fifteen classrooms. This was due to high winds, problems with water supply and construction. The cost was over £1M.

Opposite Far Left: **C.L.A.S.P.** (Consortium of Local Authorities Special Program) construction was part of the problem. A test rig shows flames spreading up the inside of the wall & across the ceiling unseen by the occupants of the classroom. A similar situation was met by firefighters tackling the blaze.

Opposite Left: **CFO Watters** speaks on the 'World in Action' TV programme. He outlined the dangers of CLASP construction and the need for fire compartmentation to prevent the rapid spread of fire. This was later fitted to buildings of this type.

Above: **Woodwork Classroom.** One of the fifteen destroyed in the Usworth School fire. Insulating materials from the ceiling lie across benches. Fire spread unchecked due to a lack of fire stopping in the common roof void.

Above: **Whirlpools:** L-Malcolm McDonald R-New Dennis TL.

Above: **Dennis Fire Appliance.** GOLF 01 outside the old Wallsend fire station. On the roof is a fixed monitor, a feature of these early Tyne & Wear appliances. A hose reel can be seen at the rear, lockers are hinged upward opening door types. The Dennis F131 became the standard fleet appliance of the 70's. Wallsend fire Stn mid 70's.

Above: **Merryweather Marquis.** Carrying a 50ft wheeled escape and still wearing a Sunderland badge. Charlie collier instructs trainees in resuscitation equipment. (Automan) *Above Right:* **T&W Tunic Button.**

Above & Below: **Telephone Exchange.** Sunderland, October, 1974. The building housing the exchange was destroyed due to an explosion. Flames still burn inside as covering jets protect adjacent property. –See petrol station below. Note: Sunderland's 'No3' appliance still has a bell and wooden 'Ajax' ladder.

Above: **White Watch.** On the roof of Stn NOVEMBER, Sunderland.

Above: **Stack Fire.** Peter Stronach with the 'new' high pressure hose reel gun fitted to new appliances. Hay bales were often set alight and were a drain on the Brigade's time and resources. Stn OSCAR. (Grindon).

Opposite Right: **Metro Incident.** Grey Street, Newcastle, April 1976. An explosion at the underground workings for the new Metro system made search & rescue operations difficult. The picture shows a rescued tunnel worker about to be raised to the surface in a skip by crane. Front cover is of 'FIRE' magazine which featured the full story by CFO Watters.

Above: Picture shows '**Forward Control**' at the entrance to the tunnel airlock. The workings were pressurized to 7PSI (0.5 bar) to keep water out. This created problems with BA (Breathing Apparatus) set duration. Also, it was 2,250ft (690M) to the working face, where the explosion occurred. Bob Appleby seated far left next to Tommy Muir both of White Watch VICTOR (Gateshead fire Station).

Above: **Whirlpools** Dec75 Santa, Jan 77 Metro Centre, Summer 76 Party.

UNISAF HOUSE
33-34 DUDLEY ROAD
TUNBRIDGE WELLS
KENT . ENGLAND TN1 1LH

VOLUME 69   No. 854   AUGUST 1976   PRICE 48p

FIRE

THE JOURNAL OF THE FIRE PROTECTION PROFESSION
INCORPORATING "INDUSTRIAL HAZARDS AND FIRE PREVENTION" AND "FIRE PICTORIAL"

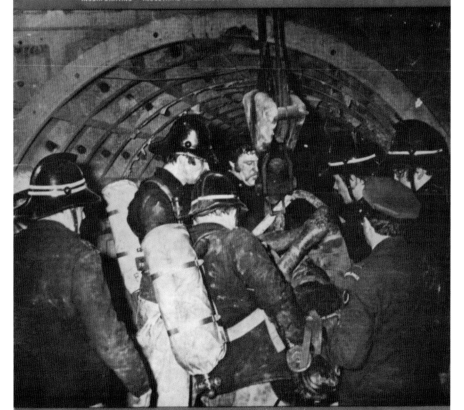

Chubb Fire

Chubb Fire are a fire consultancy, advisory bureau,
producer of the world's greatest range of fire
protection equipment and nationwide after sales
servicing organisation – with fourteen regional centres
that are fully autonomous.

**Chubb Fire
Security Ltd.,**
Pyrene House,
Sunbury-on-Thames,
Middlesex,
Telephone 85588

Above: **Metro Incident.** - Picture shows a seriously injured worker being manhandled back from the airlock to the vertical access shaft. Six persons were trapped, two died. The cause was thought to be a leak from an LPG (liquefied petroleum gas) cylinder punctured by a locomotive, which had been ignited.

Below Left: **Rescue.** Casualty is removed via crane 'basket' and hauled to the top of the shaft.

Below Right: **'Ben Fund' Badge.** The Benevolent Fund was the forerunner of The Firefighters Charity.

30

Above: **Work wear.** Stn NOVEMBER, Sunderland, 1976.
Blue nylon jackets are the issue for 'dirty jobs'. Crew stand in front of
November 03 an AEC TL, on the access road to the station forecourt.

Below: **Stn NOVEMBER** appliance line-up, Sunderland, 1970s.

Above: **Morris's.** 'FIRE' Aug 1975, 16 pumps, view looking up High St.

Above Left: **Morris's Warehouse.** 2 TL's & HP, 80 firemen, heavily smoke logged & packed with furniture & carpets, Sunderland 1975.
Above Right: **Christmas Hampers** for widows & ex-firemen, Pilgrim St.

Below: **STATION INSPECTION: 1**

ALPHA (Newburn)

BRAVO (West End)

FOXTROT (Fossway)

GOLF (Wallsend)

HOTEL (Whitley Bay)

JULIET (Tynemouth)

Above: **DELTA 02 50' HP.** 'Smoke break'. ERF Simon Snorkel with striped booms. Blue denim shirt was standard work wear issue.

Below: **BA Training School.** Tynemouth, Mick Balance & Peter Butterworth in early Draeger Normalair sets & metropolitan helmets.

Above: **Sunderland Shipbuilders.** North Sands, Mar 1977. A ship under construction at Sunderland Shipbuilders Ltd, North Sands Yard, was involved in an incident when the keel blocks caught fire. It took 15 Pumps, a TL, ET and a FoT, with 150 personnel, 36 hours to extinguish.

Above: **Tanker Fire.** Washington, Mar 1977. The OiC feels the tank side for heat as a cooling jet is applied. A foam blanket has been laid.

Above & Below Left: **Graham Gratrix.** Builders merchant, High St, Sunderland, Oct 1977. Evacuation: TL about to strike through the roof. *Below Right:* **Strike Poster.** A placard carried during strike marches.

PAY THE FIREMEN

Above: **Gordon Honeycombe.** Strike Supporter, Stn DELTA, Nov 1977. L to R - W. Davies, Dave Clark, W.Lynch, (GH), W. Wood. During the firemen's strike Gordon Honeycombe came to the North East to show his support. A regular newsreader on the ITV channel he is shown with the 'untouchable' TL that was taken to an incident.

Above: **FBU Card - Picket Badge - Green Goddess**. Firemen's Strike, '77

Above: **Discount for Beauty / Zhivagos.** High Street West, Sunderland, January 1979. A major blaze on the high street in the town centre. The shop front has completely blown out onto the pavement. The fire quickly spread to involve the night club above. Jets are directed at the first floor in an attempt to contain it.

Opposite: **Later** in the incident. The 50ft HP (Hydraulic Platform) cage closes into the nightclub's upstairs windows directing a monitor. Jets on the ground floor advance to hit stock still burning in the rear of the store.

BA (Breathing Apparatus) crews unseen inside are advancing up the stairs from the ground to the first floor nightclub.

The Dodge HP appliance shown is the same one seen airborne at the airport earlier.

Although extensively damaged, crews managed to contain the blaze to the central block and prevent spread along the entire street.

Above: **Wills Factory Tactical Exercise.** Tynemouth, June 1979.

Above: **Drills.** Stn yard, Juliet, Tynemouth, June, 1979. The Dennis roof monitor provides a jet while the TL attacks the top floor of the drill tower. Essential duties to maintain the skills of the modern firefighter.

Above: **Get Yer Hair Cut.** Recruits at Fulwell, Sunderland, Stn MIKE.
Below: **'Chamber Pots'.** Recruits wear the civil defence helmet soon replaced by the 'metropolitan' type. A young Joe Beston at back left.

Above: **A Yank But Not At Yankee.** 'Ritchie' Banaciski, was an ex-New York fireman in the brigade. Dressed in American helmet & kit, at the controls of a pump. Whirlpool No.2, Brigade magazine, Spring 1975.

Above Left: **New York Fire Department.**
Above Right: **Fire Marshal Badge.**

Above: **Charity Fire Engine Pull.** Tynemouth, August 1984.

THREE

1980'S

Above: **YANKEE 02.** Dennis RS/SS series, Swalwell, September, 1989.

Above: **Cab Reader.** 'High-Tech' eighties information system. Held topographical & water supply data on cassette. 1981.

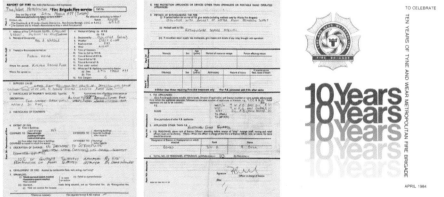

Above: **K433 Report of Fire Form**. Distinctly Low-Tech, & **10Yr Card** 84.

Opposite: **St Peters** had stood for hundreds of years when fire struck in March 1984. Nine appliances, a TL (Turntable Ladder) and ET (Emergency Tender) were required to extinguish the blaze. Here we see the initial first strike, crews were also deployed inside.

The crews are removing slates to gain access to the roof fire. Apart from the fire there was also a danger from the very large falling slates and molten lead from the roof flashings. Arson was suspected.

St Peter's Church. Monkwearmouth, Sunderland, March, 1984.
45′ (13.5M) ladders deployed for roof access.

Above: **A690 Chemical Incident.** Durham Road, Sunderland, March 1980. Toluene & plastic monomers involved, chemical suits in use.

Above: **First Aid Champions.** Tommy Taylor & Graeme Bowser receive the CFOA district award from CFO Richard Bull, 1987.

Below: **STATION INSPECTION: 2**

KILO (South Shields)

LIMA (River Station)

MIKE (Fulwell)

NOVEMBER (Sunderland Central)

OSCAR (Grindon)

ROMEO (Tunstall)

Above: **Tree Blown Over**

Above: **House Fire**

The **Back** of the premises later in the incident. Most of the ridge line has been removed with large quantities of thatch in the yard. The cause is thought to have been a spark from the chimney of the coal-fired living room. Ladders both 45' (13.5M) and 35' (10.5M) deployed.

The incident was not one of the more 'routine' jobs that the Brigade normally responds to. This thatched cottage with its roof on fire provided a new experience for the crews involved. Having stood for nearly 100 years the thatch was nearly 3 feet thick. Much of had to be removed to extinguish a deep seated fire.

Opposite Above: Here we see the pump deployed with numerous hose lines and hosereels in action. Careful use of water is required to prevent damage to rooms below. Work required the use of hay forks which had to be delivered in large numbers.

Not an incident that many of the crews attending thought that they would ever 'turn-out' to, at least not in an urban brigade area.

Thatched Cottage. Cleadon, Sunderland, August 1981.

Above: **Turntable Ladder** is deployed as a water tower. Water is directed onto the roof of the cylinder store section to prevent spread to that area. This shot shows the rear of the building. Former windows have been sealed with breeze blocks in an attempt to prevent vandalism and break-ins. This made access to the fire more difficult for the fire brigade.

Top Right: Newbottle Co-oP burns fiercely as crews battle in a forlorn hope of saving part of the building. 8 Pumps and 2 Turntable Ladders with a Command Unit attended the blaze. The building was used as a depot for the Co-oP's TV repair service. A fire brigade spokesman described the two storey building to 'The Journal' newspaper as "well alight".

Bottom Right: **Jets** are deployed on the frontage in an attempt to prevent spread. The building was already engulfed in flame when crews arrived and they had little chance of reducing damage. The section to the left was found to have a store of acetylene cylinders, which is where most of the firefighting operations were directed, until removed.

Above: **Newbottle Co-oP.** Houghton-Le-Spring, January 1984.

Above: **Pylon Special Service.** Washington, August 1986. Crews involved in a pylon rescue were awarded medals for their actions. L-R Lenny Lowther, Colin Adamson, Frankie Duckworth, John Mair, John Thornaby, Graham Whitfield, John Bates, Graham Aitken.

Above Left: **Tyne & Wear Bravery Award Medal.**
Above Centre: **Queens Gallantry Medal.**
Above Right: **High Voltage Electricity Pylon.** Washington Highway. During the incident there was a very real threat of electrocution and thus risk to life.

TOOLS OF THE TRADE - BRANCHES

1. The **Type 'A'** - chromed

2. The **Noble**

3. The **London**

4. The **Noble** in action sans helmet

5. The **Nap4** and in action – Chopwell Woods 6.

7. **Akron** HR gun.

8. The **Gilmat**

9. New Variable Flow type **AWG.**

The 'Branchpipe' gives manual control of water flow as Jet or Spray.

Above: **Car Fire ECHO 02.** Motorway, Newcastle, January, 1988.

Above: **Brigade Pipe Band.** Formed for use on ceremonial occasions, such as medal presentations and remembrance services. Alex Fairgrieve arranged continental tours such as Ypres. 1989.

Above: **Volvo Appliance.** JULIET 01, Tynemouth, January, 1988

Above: **Command Unit.** Derek Dunwoodie, ALPHA, Newcastle, 1982.

Above: **Diggers.** Crews standby while JCBs widen the trench.

While a workman was laying drainage pipes in an unshuttered trench the walls collapsed onto him. JCB diggers were required to move a large amount of soil to gain access. Firefighters then had to remove the final few feet by hand to remove the body. Trench was to the left of the station (below) on a grassed area adjacent the drill yard. Incident began with dayshift crews (R/W) and ended with nightshift (W/W) finally completing the task.

Above: **Stn ROMEO.** Tunstall Fire Station, Sunderland.

Trench Collapse. Tunstall Fire Station, Sunderland, April, 1989.
Below: **Access.** Crews move in to remove the last few feet of soil.

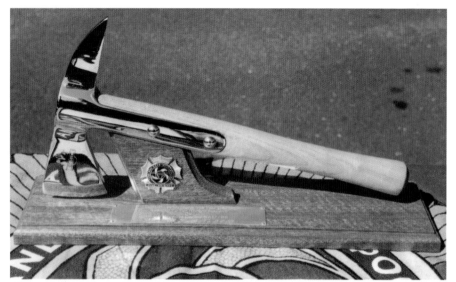

Above: **The Silver Axe.** Training School, South Shields, December, 1989.

Above: **Award Ceremony.** Training School, South Shields, 1989.

Above: **HMI Inspection.** New recruits, South Shields, September, 1987.

Above: **GMC Rescue Tender.** T08, Hebburn Fire Station, April, 1989.

Above Left: **Fire Engine Pull.** Dennis & gorilla, Newcastle, 1988.
Above Right: **Decontam Shower.** Tactical Exercise, chemical suit, 1989.

Below: **STATION INSPECTION: 3**

SIERRA (Washington)

TANGO (Hebburn)

VICTOR (Gateshead)

WHISKEY (Birtley)

YANKEE (Swalwell)

ZULU (Chopwell)

Opposite Below: **New Brigade Control Centre.** West Denton, Newcastle, a relocation from Pilgrim St. Opened by HRH Duke of Kent, Nov, 1987.

Above: **Overturned Appliance.** Sunderland, 1989.

Above: **Old Dennis Appliances.** Ready for disposal, Stn BRAVO.

Above: **New GOLF.** (Wallsend) fire station, March, 1989.

Above: **Party Time.** For the New GOLF, staff old & new.

*Left:***Wallsendcake&Boardgames**?

Above: **Field Fire.** A common event for firefighters in the summer.

Above: **20 Year Medal Ceremony.** Alex Fairgrieve receives award for exemplary service. ALPHA, West Denton, Newcastle, September, 1989.

Above: **Fire Engine Pull.** Fawcett Street, Sunderland, April, 1980. L-R alternately, Keith Attwell, Dave Hodgson, Norman Williamson, Alan Bailey, Harry Moir, Graeme French, John Flynn, Author, Bill Langton, Bernie Tully. Dave Bark at right provides the music – bagpipes.

Above: **ROMEO White.** L-R Martin Stuthridge, Ron Hodgkinson, Ritchie Reah, Peter Hewitson, Bernie Tully, Author, Alan Hood, Terry Havenhand, Ron McMurrough. In the quadrangle at Tunstall. S/lnd.

Above Right: **HP Wall Plaque.** Collectable memorabilia.

Opposite Bottom: **Fireboat.** Vedra, based at Sunderland (November). Tinea was at Fossway (Foxtrot). They were towed by the new 'Rapid Intervention' Vehicles – emergency tenders. June, 1990

Above: **BA Team Group** G/W JULIET, North Shields, June, 1990. L to R Gordon Smith, Peter Smith, Dave Walton, Tony Wood, Ken Wilson, Steve Clark, John Porterfield. Factory unit fire, East George Street.

FOUR

1990'S

Opposite: The Suite Centre in Toward Road, Sunderland, was the scene of a major fire on 12th December 1991. 8 Pumps, 2 TL's, (Turntable Ladder) the ICU (Incident Command Unit) and ST (Salvage Tender) were deployed. Picture shows TL in action as a water tower directing a jet onto upper floors.

The store was full of furniture and bedding, heavy smoke logging hampered operations. The rescue cage of the TL can be seen stowed to the right of the main ladder, dirt from the roads covers the bodywork.

Bottom Right: Picture shows jets being directed to upper floors from the ground. Pump (ROMEO 02) is used as base pump for TL water tower operation. Ladder - 35' also in position for access to upper balcony.

Bottom Left: TL operator in conference with Officer in Charge as to next requirements. Monitor operator is descending ladder as water tower operations are completed. Another 35' extension ladder is deployed on this side of the building.

Above: **SCS Sunderland Suite Centre.** Toward Road, Sunderland, December 1991.

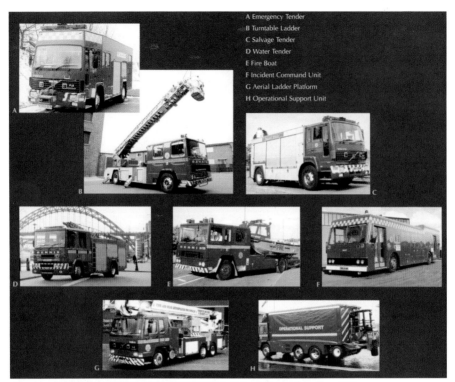

A Emergency Tender
B Turntable Ladder
C Salvage Tender
D Water Tender
E Fire Boat
F Incident Command Unit
G Aerial Ladder Platform
H Operational Support Unit

Above: **APPLIANCE INSPECTION.** Machines for the 90's.

Above: **New ECHO.** (Gosforth) fire station, April, 1990.

Above: **Ops Servicing.** Mick Tibbs maintaining BA on the test box.
Above Right: **Diktron DSUs.** Distress Signal Units used with BA sets.

68

Above: **New A.L.P.** In action. Factory unit fire, July, 1991.

Above: **RIOTS.** A pub burns out of control, September, 1991.
Right: **Bricked.** DELTA 02 bears the battle scars of the nights of unrest.
Below: **RIOTS.** Shop units, fire contained, police in attendance. 1991.

Above: **RIOTS.** The Meadowell and West End burn. Tyneside, 1991.
Below: **Collingwood Youth Centre** blazes in the night.

Above: **RIOTS.** Police in riot gear protect firemen. Flash hoods donned.

```
14/09/91 0155 1631    VDU 0
TITLE:   TO ALL PERSONNEL FROM ACO BREMNER.

ACO BREMNER WISHES TO THANK EVERYONE FOR THEIR COMMITMENT, DEDICATION AND
ASSISTANCE DURING THE PAST NINE HOURS.
DUE TO YOUR EFFORTS WE HAVE ATTENDED EVERY FIRE WHICH HAS REQUIRED OUR
ATTENDANCE WITH ONLY ONE FIREFIGHTER INJURED.
```

Below: **Aftermath.** Gutted buildings line the road.

Above: **Factory Fire.** Gateshead, August, 1991.

BRIGADE AREA AND HEADQUARTERS

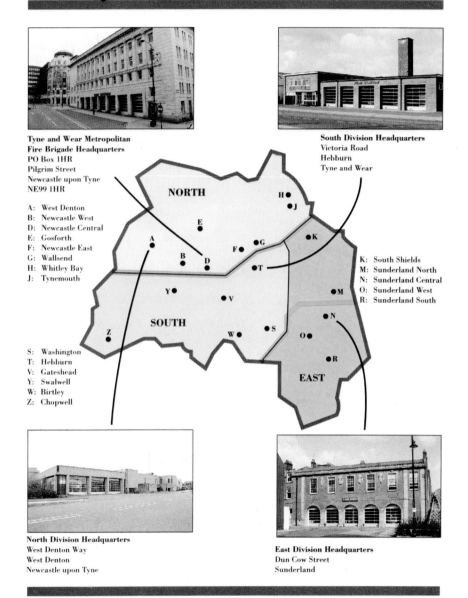

Tyne and Wear Metropolitan
Fire Brigade Headquarters
PO Box 1HR
Pilgrim Street
Newcastle upon Tyne
NE99 1HR

A: West Denton
B: Newcastle West
D: Newcastle Central
E: Gosforth
F: Newcastle East
G: Wallsend
H: Whitley Bay
J: Tynemouth

South Division Headquarters
Victoria Road
Hebburn
Tyne and Wear

K: South Shields
M: Sunderland North
N: Sunderland Central
O: Sunderland West
R: Sunderland South

S: Washington
T: Hebburn
V: Gateshead
Y: Swalwell
W: Birtley
Z: Chopwell

North Division Headquarters
West Denton Way
West Denton
Newcastle upon Tyne

East Division Headquarters
Dun Cow Street
Sunderland

NORTH

SOUTH

EAST

Above: Behind the tanker is a line of parked cars, these became involved when the running petrol fire spread. An initial foam attack can be seen.

Above: Newcastle Road. Appliances are deployed and covering jets in place. A black pall of smoke is blown east over the swimming baths. To the right is Priory car showroom. A police car blocks access to the incident.

Above: **Petrol Tanker Fire.** Newcastle Road, Sunderland, August, 1992. 34,000 litres of petrol were released when a tanker collided with a minibus, causing it to overturn and catch fire. All tanks became involved and a running petrol fire developed. 14 appliances were needed to control the blaze using 13,000 litres of foam.

Above: Firefighters clear the debris from the tanks.

1.   11.37 2.   11.38

3.   11.43 4.

5.   6.

Above: **Petrol Tanker Fire.-Video Stills.** - Taken from a training film made from footage shot during the incident.

1 to 3 shows timings of attack and eventual success.

4. - Earlier, an attack from the other side.

5. - Aerial shot from the police helicopter.

6. - Mop up, as shell of tanker is lifted away by a crane.

Above Left: **Cross House Fire Re-Enactment.** 'Ian & Tommy' receive medals from CFO Richard Bull. Westgate Road, Newcastle, 1994. Fireman Thomas Brown received the Albert Medal for his part in the real rescues. Re-enactment was 75th anniversary of event.

Above Right: **Brass Fireman's Helmet.** An antique piece of headgear in use at the time of the original fire (1919).

Above: **Dennis F12.** The Brigade's vintage pump used in rescues for the re-enactment, with wheeled escape. Cross House behind.

Above: This shot is taken diametrically opposite the lead picture. It shows just how close the adjacent tanks are, and how they are at risk from considerable radiated heat. A major effort was directed at protecting surrounding risks and preventing the tank itself from collapse by heat and flame. Orange lights are street lights

Opposite: A Gas Storage tank at Dunston (Gateshead) is involved in fire as its contents burns fiercely. The cause being a suspected explosive device planted by terrorist organization(s) - (IRA). 2 Million cubic feet of natural gas was ignited and 20 appliances tackled the blaze, containing the fire to the tank of origin.

Above: **Gas Tank.** Dunston, Gateshead, June, 1993.

Above & Opposite: **IRD.** Fossway, Newcastle, March 1994. 14 appliances fight to control a fire in the large multi-storey building. It was confined to three floors but was assessed as costing £11M. in damages.

Above: **Technical Quiz.** Team winners from ROMEO. L-R Jeff Foster, Steve Anderson, Ritchie Tough, Trevor Smith, Warren Mulvaney. Held every year between stations to improve technical knowledge, 1990.

Opposite & Above: **Train Station.** Newcastle, March, 1995. Fire in the roof, caused by repair work. Crews confine it to that area but disruption is caused as trains are diverted. Platforms provide access.

Above: **Bronto Skylift.** Aerial Ladder Platform, Workshops, 1995.

Vacant Factory. Gateshead, 15 pumps & 70 firefighters, March 1996.

Above: **Fire screen.** G/W YANKEE, Newcastle Airport, February, 1995. Crews in the act of 'valving down' a flammable liquid fire.

Above: **R.V.P.** Newcastle Airport, February, 1995. Appliances ready for a 'Le-Mans' style start to a tactical exercise. Gill Air aircraft at rear.

Above: Looking South from the TL cage. The other TL can be seen in the distance at the opposite end. Monitor (branch) is on the right, its discharge of water set to a trickle to allow an unobscured camera shot. The full extent of the damage can be seen from this angle, with most of the roof destroyed.

Opposite Above: Flames just start to break through the roof of the Tynemouth Plaza. This view, looking North, shows a ladder deployed to the left. Officers, on the right, are doing a reconnaissance of the building perimeter to see the extent of fire spread.

Opposite Below: deployment of appliances on Grand Parade. Two TL's (Turntable Ladders) are being used as water towers at either end. The far right of the building is the end structure of the opposite above picture. OiC relays instructions via pocket set radio.

Tynemouth Plaza. Grand Parade, Tynemouth, February, 1996. Incident required 12 Pumps, 3 TL's, ICU, ET, & ST.

Above: **Tynemouth Plaza.** Daylight reveals the extent of the damage.

Above: **KILO Volvo Line-up.** Two Pumps & ET at South Shields.

5. **PBI Gold** - Ritchie Reah & Alan Hood   6.   7.

Above: **1**. Early 70s, Ian Hunter **2**. Nomex, Gary Yates **3**. The London Way, Paul Walmsley **4**. The 60s, Dave Garrett **6**. 'Undress' uniform - Gavin Briggs, & **7**. The female 'Control' version, Chris Kennedy.

DRESS OF THE DAY - FIREKIT & UNDRESS

Above: Derelict warehouse, well alight. Spectacular flames & smoke leap skyward while TLs and jets attack. Unfortunately this was not the only time that the Brigade had to attend such fires in this area.

Above: **DELTA 04** Emergency Tender, Pilgrim St, Newcastle, 1994.

Warehouse Fire. Quayside, Newcastle, February, 1997.

Above Left: **Joe Nevison.** The 'Man with the Camera'. Often at fires & social events as the Brigade photographer. Sadly past away 2009.

Above: **New NOVEMBER.** Sunderland Central, Railway Row, 1993.

Above: **Three Wise Men.** Dick Allen, Ray Hughes & Alan Holmes consult as to the best plan of action. Senior officers in command.
Below: The full extent of the fire can be seen from this distance shot. Caused by arson, the fire is well developed when appliances arrive.

Above: **Make Up.** Crews maintain & re-stow equipment on appliances. Entrance to market on left, Grey's monument in background.

Below: **TL.** 100ft ladder is made ready. Smoke still issuing from front.

Grainger Market Newcastle, March, 1998. Roof damage is evident as officers asses post fire operations. The clean up begins.

Above: **Car Fire.** The cause of numerous firecalls, often arson.

Above: **Action Stations.** Durham Fire Brigade In-house magazine. A cross border incident in the County's area. T&W assist under Sec12. – the mutual assistance scheme. Burning cables, Burnhopefield, 1991.

Left: **25 Year FBU Badge.** Alan Hood receives his badge from Fire Brigades Union Representative Gordon Chalk. Station ROMEO, (Tunstall), Sunderland.

Above Right: **Seaburn Fire Engine Rally.** Organised by Ron Hodgkinson, an annual event for some years, cover shows the late Dennis Barker's Blackburn appliance.

Above: **Dennis Sabre.** Stn BRAVO, Newcastle, May, 1998.

Above Left: **Bob Foster & Star.** Arson investigation team, Feb, 1998.
Above Right: **Dr Douglas.** Long-time Brigade medical specialist.

Above: **Brigade Training Centre.** Barmston Mere, Washington, October, 1996. Taken from the TL cage. Drills in progress, Nissan autos at rear.

Above: **Chernobyl Tribute.** Stn DELTA, Newcastle, 1995. The Brigade was host to an artist whose work was placed on the roof of headquarters. Portraits of the Russian firefighters who died preventing the Chernobyl disaster becoming much worse. Banner portraits to right. Later the Brigade hosted visits from the children of the area.

Above: **Oval Community Centre.** Stn SIERRA, Washington, July, 1996.

Above: **Chip Pan Demonstration.** Stn JULIET, Tynemouth, May, 2001.

Above: **AEC Regent.** Stn KILO, South Shields, (closure), May, 2001.

Opposite Above: An incident of 'Just Wood' that tied up the resources of the Brigade for a number of days. It was in fact the name of a recycling wood plant that used scrap wood as base material. 18 Pumps, 2 ALPs, TL, ET, OSU attended.

Opposite Below: Here the scale of the incident can be seen. Flames rise above the complete horizon. A lone ALP (Aerial Ladder Platform) - battles on against a sea of flame in this sector of the incident.

Above: **Jets.** Evidence that the author did actually do some 'work' during service. Ade Usher to right.

Above: **RTA (Road Traffic Accident) Tyne Tunnel.** 2001.

104

Just Wood. Wallsend, Newcastle, May, 2001. Mick English issues commands via a radio handset as he patrols the perimeter.

Opposite Above: Flames vent through the roof of the Thorn-Holmeserve factory on the Boldon Industrial Estate, Sunderland. Crews get to work on the initial deployment of covering jets. The building is already well alight at this early stage and the chances of saving it are remote. A ground monitor is stationed at the far left to try and prevent fire spread. 6 Pumps, 2 ALPs, (Aerial Ladder Platforms) a Control Unit and Emergency Tender attend.

Opposite Below: The initial attendance from Station MIKE (Fulwell) gets to work at the front of the building. The cage of the ALP can be seen on the left moving towards the centre. Jets are deployed working through the office section of the factory.

*Above:***Remembrance.**Brigade contingent at war memorial, Sunderland.
Below Left: **Wreaths.** Fire Brigade and associations. 9-11 remembrance.
Below Right: **Parade.** All services unite to honour the fallen.

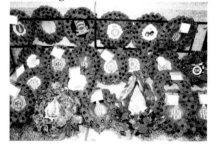 

Thorn-Holmeserve. Boldon, Sunderland, June, 2001.

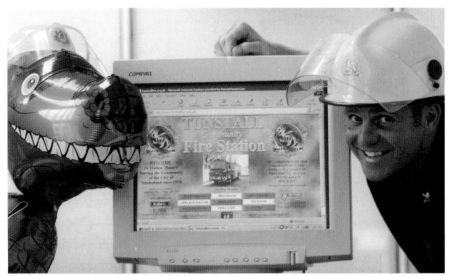

Stn Website. Tunstall, Kev Sirey & 'Rex' launch the first fire Stn community website for ROMEO-Tunstall, Sunderland, April, 2001.

Chernobyl Children. Russian kids visit ALPHA on a visit. L-R Gary Miller, Keith Bell, Dave Turner, Dave Kieernan, Mick Mahon, Gary Yates, Glen Ryan.

Gas Explosion. North Shields, June, 2001. A house totally destroyed.

Opposite Above: The smoke plume could be seen from over ten miles away from the Distillex fire. A site for recycling industrial solvents and chemicals this made it an extremely hazardous incident.This view shows the cloud drifting south over Tyne & Wear from a point upstream on the river Tyne. A total of 16 pumping appliances were required, with backup from both Durham and Northumberland fire services.

Opposite Below: Here we see a close up of the scene during clearance operations. Large storage tanks in the background were covered by ground monitors so preventing explosion. Not so with the large number of storage drums (foreground) which became high velocity projectiles, some landing streets away from the incident. Also note gas cylinders to the left, more potential bombs. Contents from leaking drums caused a running flammable liquid fire, which spread rapidly throughout the site.

Above: **Volvo Emergency 1.** Stn GOLF, Newcastle, June, 2001.

Distillex, North Shields, Tyneside, April, 2002.

Above: **AEC Turntable Ladder CFT801D.** The same TL on page 62 being sold off. Now owned by Phil Davison, on show at Preston Park.

Above: **ERF Pump PFT117L.** Another ex-Tynemouth machine.
Both appliances in a fine state of preservation due to the dedication and hard work of their owners.

Above: **Regents View.** Aged Persons Home, Hetton-Le-Hole, October, 2002. A fire destroys the mid section of the roof, crews prevent spread.

Above: **Young Firefighters.** Santa is assisted and at the same time funds raised for The Firefighters Charity, City Centre, Sunderland

FIRE HELMETS 1974 - 2004

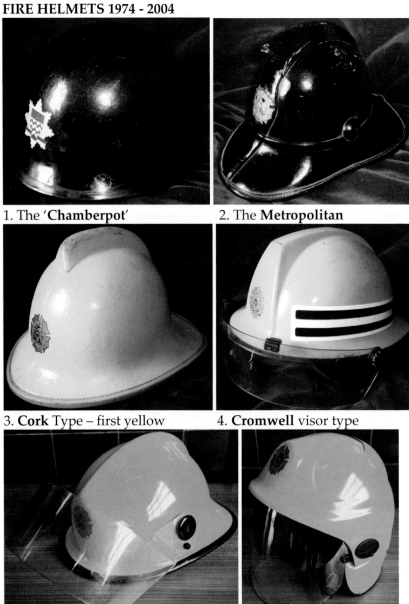

1. The **'Chamberpot'**

2. The **Metropolitan**

3. **Cork** Type – first yellow

4. **Cromwell** visor type

5. **Pacific** type visor 2

6. **Gallet** type Cromwell

7. **Brass** type   8. **American** type

Above & Below: **New Stations: QUEBEC.** North Moor, Sunderland. In reality it could be any of the new stations - the 'standard' Stn realised.

PFI (Private Finance Initiative) stations replaced the oldest building stock throughout the service. This led to a series of closing events in which staff who had served on old stations attended farewell tours. Some, even from the time of the 1960's and beyond. Progress.

CHIEF FIRE OFFICERS 1978 - 2007

M. Armstrong M.B.E. F.I.Fire E.
Chief Fire Officer 1978 - 1981

J.F. Elton O.B.E. Q.F.S.M. F.I.Fire E.
Chief Fire Officer 1981 - 1991

W.W. Dunlop O.B.E. Q.F.S.M. F.I.Fire E.
Chief Fire Officer 1991 - 1995

R. Bull A.I.Fire E.
Chief Fire Officer 1995 -

Above: **Old VICTOR.** Gateshead, closes, rebuilt on same site, 2005. Staff old and new say goodbye to stations they have served on.

*Above:***Old FOXTROT.**Fossway, Newcastle, drill yard, November, 2006.

118

Win a Silver Axe

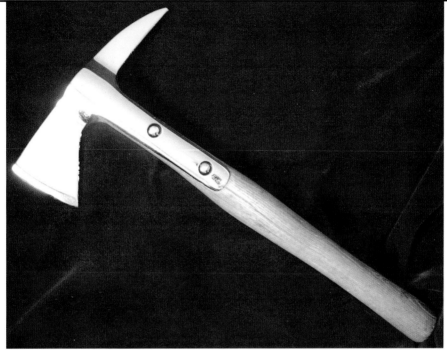

Above: **Win a Silver Axe** like the one above by entering our free draw. Go to our website at www.twfire.com and enter your reference number K433999. (Terms & Conditions Apply) To be drawn by a fire service celebrity. Good Luck.

By purchasing this book you have also made a donation to The Fire Fighters Charity, which assists firefighters & their families in time of need.

NOTE: The 'Silver Axe' is actually a chrome-nickel coated steel bladed tool. The name comes from the award given to the best recruit of the firefighters initial course. (It is *not* made of real silver).

SURNAME FORENAME **A** Abbott Martin Ackinclose Charles Adam Alistair Adamopoulos Alex Adams Gwen Adams Paul Adamson Colin Adamson John Addison Peter Addison Keith Agar George Agnew John Ahmed Philip Ahmed Paul Ahmed Peter Ahmed Peter Ahmed Peter Ainslie Michael Aird Geoffrey Aisbitt Albert Aitken Graham Akroyd Patricia Alderson Albert Alderson Eric Alderson David Allan Richard Allan Angela Allen Frederick Allen Philip Allen Tony Allfree Mark Allison Neil Allison Howard Allison John Allpress George Allsop Ian Allsop Debra Allsop Ian Allsopp David Allsopp David Anderson Robert Anderson Geoffrey Anderson Paul Anderson Jeffrey Anderson Beth Anderson Jon Anderson Jon Anderson Stephen Anderson Paul Anderson Richard Anderson Paul Anderson Roderick Anderson Steven Anderson Jon J Anderson Neil Anderson Wayne Anderson Ian Angus Ian Anthony Harold Appleby Robert Appleby Philip Appleby Andrew Appleby Stuart Arbuthnot Kevin Archer Hilton Armitage Ronald Armstrong John Armstrong Peter Armstrong Richard Armstrong William Armstrong Thomas Armstrong Maurice Arnopp Michael Arnott George Asbury Martin Ashbridge William Ashbridge Douglas Ashman Howard Ashman Darin Askell Norman Askew John Astley Gavin Athey Richard Atkinson Robert Atkinson Stephen Attwell Keith Austin Victor Austin Anthony **B** Bachurzewski Paul Backhurst Christopher Bagnall Paul Bailey Alan Bailey John Bailey Kenneth Bailey Raymond Bain Edward Baines Frederick Baines John Baird Austin Baird Stephen Baitey Alan Baker Harry Baker Peter Baker Derek Ball Kenneth Ball Rebekah Ballance Michael Bannan Paul Barber George Barber William Barber Andrew Bark David Bark Calum Barker Dennis Barnes Thomas Barnes Neil Tatem Barnes David Barnes David Barnes David Barnfather Ian Barr Peter Barratclough Albert Barrett Brian Barrett David Barrow Alan Barrow Paul Barten Nicolaes Barton Mark Bartram Daren Bate James Bate John Bathgate Iain Battle Michael Baxter Kenneth Bays Andrew Beardsmore Angus Bedlington John Bell James Bell Colin Bell John Bell Kenneth Bell David Bell Carl Bell David Bell Robert Bell Gerald Bell Keith Bell Ian Bell Lee Bell Howard Bell David Bell Duncan Belshaw Julie Belshaw John Bennett Thomas Bennett Keith Benson Paul Bentham Claire Bernard George Bertram Donald Berwick David Best David Best Stephen Best Alan Beston Joseph Betteridge Carol Bettis Stephen Bevan Gary Bewick Steven Bewick Charles Bickle Peter Bickle Anthony Bickle Scott Biggs Gavin Biggs Richard Bilcliffe Thomas Binns Michael Binyon George Birch Thomas Bird Anthony Bird Anthony Birrell William Bishop Howard Black Jeffrey Black Ian Black Robert Blackett Adrian Blackett David Blackett Paul Blacklock Peter Blackwell Frank Blair Robert Blakely David Blakey Frederick Blakey Ian Blenkinsop Robert Blenkinsop Ian Blenkiron Kenneth Blenkiron Alan Blower Ian Blower Andrew Blyth David Bodden Jeremy Boddy Darren Bolam Philip Bonar Andrew Bone Paul Booth Frank Borgesson Carl Borsberry Neil Borthwick Martin Bosher Ronald Bosher Alan Boucher Arthur Bourne Christine Bowker Mark Bowmaker John Bowman George Bowman James Bowman Colin Bowser Graeme Boyack David Boyd Michael Boyd Denise Boyd Michael Boyd Paul Boyd Damian Boyes Martin Boyle Shaun Braby Arthur Bracchi Kevin Bradley Craig Brady James Brailsford John Bramfitt William Branch Malcolm Brandon Eric Brannen Jason Brayson James Brayson Michael Breeden Graham Breeden Geoffrey Breeze Gerald Bremner James Bremner Ian Brew Anthony Brewer Gary Briganti Lisa Briggs George Bright John Brisbane Walter Broadbent Donald Broadbent Mary Broderick Keith Brookbanks Philip Brooks James Brotherton Grant Brown David Brown George Brown John Brown John Brown Anthony Brown Stephen Brown George Brown Ian Brown Paul Brown James Brown David Brown Alan Brown David Brown Adrian Brown Paul Brown Steven Brown Preston Brown Jason Browne Clinton Brownson Michael Brownson Paul Bruce David Bruce Andrew Brunton Luca Bryce James Buchanan Ian Buchanan Amanda Buchanan Robert Buckett Alan Bull Richard Bulmer Nigel Bunbury Michael Burchat John Burdis Stephen Burke Tom Burke John Burke John Burke Christopher Burness William Burnett Neil Burnip Grahame Burns James

120

Burns Kevin Burns Steven Burton Christopher Bushell Christopher Butler Graham Butterworth Peter Buxton David Byrne Owen $\boxed{C}$ Cairns Edward Caisley Carolyne Calder Graeme Cameron Keith Cameron Susan Cameron Keith Campbell Robert Campbell Thomas Campbell Peter Canham Gary Capeling Thomas Carabine Gary Carlington Kevin Carney David Carr John Carr William Carr Robert Carr Darren Carr James Carroll Neil John Carroll James Carruthers Scott Carruthers Keith Carson Alan Carss Barry Carter Susan Cartledge Frederick Cartner Trevor Cartwright Joseph Carver Peter Cass-Williams David Catchpole William Cave Michael Caygill Steven Cessford Trevor Chadkirk Derek Chalk Gordon Chalk Steven Chambers Stephen Chape Lee Chapman Anthony Charlton William Charlton Thomas Charlton Gerard Charlton Andrew Charlton Neville Charlton Lisa Chisholm Brian Chisholm Christine Christie Keith Clapperton Joseph Clark James Clark David Clark Barry Clark Derek Clark Alison Clark Alison Clark James Clark Andrew Clark Stephen Clark Gordon Clark Phillip Clark Andrew Clarke William Clarke Ian Clarke David Clarke David Clarke Scott Clarkson Emma Clements Scott Cloke Kenneth Close Allyson Coakley Michael Coates John Coates Hugh Cochrane Edwin Cockburn John Cockburn Anthony Cockburn Stanley Codling Michael Coleclough Alan Collier Charles Collins Victor Collins Robert Common Steven Connolly Martin Connolly Michael Conroy Allan Convery David Cook Victor Cook Christopher Cook Brian Cook Stephen Cook Jonathan Cooper John Cooper Edward Cooper Neil Cooper Paul Cooper John Copeland David Corah Peter Corbett Peter Corbett Kenneth Corbridge Robert Corbridge Peter Corner Alan 1122 Costigan John Coulthard Arnold Coulthard Mark Cowans Michael Cowans Michael Cowie Christopherjohn Cowley David Cox David Cox Thomas Cox David Coxon John Craggs Paul Craig David Craig Raymond Crann Colin Crawford Frederick Crawford Stephen Crawley Aiden Critchlow Brian Critchlow William Crookes Ian Crosier Williams Crosier Elliott Crouch John Crozier James Crutwell Ian Crutwell Kevin Cuggy Michael Cummings Arthur Cummings Joseph Curran David Curran Paul Curran Carmen Currie Matthew Curry George Curry William Curry Malcolm Curry Paul Curry Troy Curtis Malcolm Curtis Rodney Curtis David Curtis Scott Cuskin Ian Cuthbertson Garry Cutting Geoffrey $\boxed{D}$ Dabrowski Jan Dabrowski Doreen Daglish John Dance Ruth Davies Glyn Davies Glenn Davis Edward Davison William Davison George Davison Robert Davison Leslie Davison Henry Davison Deborah Davison Deborah Davison Ian Davison Rebecca Dayson Michael Deacon Stuart Dean Raymond Dean Carl Delmar George Denholm Harold Denny Lee Devlin Ronald Devon Keith Diamond Alan Dias Paul Dickinson Colin Dinning Francis Dinning Wilfred Ditch Brian Ditch Michael Dix Stephen Dix Diane Dixon Colin Dixon David Dixon David Dixon Derek Dobson George Dobson Lysa Dobson Paul Dobson Stuart Docherty Christopher Dodd Sydney Dodd Graham Dodd Mark Dodd John Dodd Leslie Dodd Gary Dodd Natalie Dodds Allen Dodds Robert Dodds Kevin Dodds Garry Dodds Ian Doig Kenneth Dolby Leonard Don Peter Don Katheleen Donnell Cathryn Donnigan Stephen Donoghue Vincent Douglas Malcolm Douglas Paul Douglas Paul Douglass William Douthwaite Paul Dove Robert Downey Alan Downey Andrew Downie Kevin Driver David Drummond Thomas Dryden John Duckworth Frank Dudding Thomas Duff Graeme Dunbar Peter Duncan Bryan Duncan Michael Dunlop William Dunn Eland Dunne Anthony Dunville James Dutton Jonathan Edgar Paul Edgar Dennis Edgar Malcolm $\boxed{E}$ Edgar Leigh Edminson Richard Edminson William Edmond Paul Edmondson Peter Edwards Gylndwr Edwards Ronald Edwards Michael Edwards Scott Edwards Gareth Elder Alexander Ellerby Steven Elliott Trevor Elliott William Elliott Norman Elliott Jane Elliott Jeffrey Elliott John Elliott Graham Ellison David Ellison Angela Ellison David Ellison David Elton Thomas Emerson John Robert Emmerson Keith Emmerson Anthony Emmerson Andrew English Michael English John English David Enright Michael Epsly George Errington Steven Escott David Etherington Michael Evans Jason $\boxed{F}$ Fahey Andrew Fairgrieve Alexander Falcus Joseph Falcus Mark Farquharson

Charles Farrell Steven Farrell Kevin Farrell Kevin Farrer Arthur Farrow Charles Farrow David
Farrow Malcolm Farrow David Farrow Charles Farthing Leslie Fay Christopher Fell Michael
Fenn Paul Fenton Darren Fenwick Brian Ferguson James Ferry John Finlay Anthony Finn
Raymond Finn Joseph Finneran Thomas Finnigan Brian Finnigan Lee Firth Geoffrey Fisher
David Fisher Colin Fisher Michael Fisher Warren Fisher Anthony Fisher Daniel Flaherty Diane
Fleming David Fleming Alan Fletcher Robert Fletcher John Flett Robert Flint Leonard Flint John
Flounders Ben Flynn John Flynn James Foley Lee Forbes Michael Ford David Ford Colin
Foreman Gary Foreman John Forrest Michael Forster John Forster Peter Forster Robert Forster
John Forster Martin Forster John Forster Ian Forster Craig Forster Keith Forster William Forster
Geoffrey Forster Lee Forster Dani John Forsyth Kate Foster Alexander Foster David Foster John
Foster Christopher Foster Frederick Foster Paul Foster Jeffrey Foster Bryan Foster Tracy Foster
Steven Fox Paul Frazer Robert French Graeme Frost Paul Fullen Katherine Fulton George Fyall
William **G** Gaffing Adrian Gall Douglas Gallagher Frederick Gallagher Terence Gardiner
Alexander Gardner Kenneth Gardner Thomas Gardner Christopher Gardner Kevin Garrett
David Garrington Stephen Garrity Anthony Garthwaite Anthony Gascoigne Alan Gash Alan
Geddis Trevor Gee Steven Gent William Gerrard Ian Gerrard Mark Ghazal Jamil Gibb Douglas
Gibbins Alan Gibbs William Gibson David Gibson Ronald Gibson Dennis Gibson Philip Gibson
Michael Gibson Nicholas Gicquel Ian Gilkerson Alan Gill David Gilligan Leslie Gilmore Wayne
Gingell Kevin Glenwright Keith Gobo Walter Golden Andrew Golightly Michael Goodman
Charles Gordon Peter Gordon George Gormley Bruce Gott Ernest Gradwell Eric Gradwell Jon
Graham David Graham Michael Graham Paul Graham Steven Graham Barry Graham Michael
Graham John Graham Lee Gransbury Peter Grant David Gray David Gray Ronald Gray Robert
Gray David Gray David Gray Jonathan Gray Steven Green John Greener Lee Greenwell Paul
Greenwell Christopher Gregg Paul Robert Gregory Paul Gregson James Griffin Terence Grimes
Anthony Grimes Edward Grimes Derek Gullon Robert Gurling Kathleen Gurling Kenneth
Gutcher Stephen Guy Edward **H** Hadfield William Hagon Geoffrey Hague Barry Haines
Trevor Hales Peter Haley Iain Halford David Halkyard Robert Hall Geoffrey Hall Charles Hall
John Hall Nigel Hall Charles Hall James Hall William Hall Keith Hall John Hall Alan Hall David
Hall Stuart Halstead Stephen Hamil Peter Hamilton David Hamilton Peter Hammond Barbara
Hancill Andrew Hancock John Hands Steven John Hands Russell Hanlon Neil Hannah Shaun
Hansell Anthony Hansen Shaun Hanson Bryn Haram Keith Harbottle Michelle Harbottle Paul
Harden John Harding Mark Hardy Scott Harle Graeme Harper George Harrington Neil Harris
John Harris William Harris Brian Harris Neville Harris Ian Harrison David Harrison John
Harrison Geoffrey Harrison Neil Harrison Edward Harrison David Hart Brian Hartley Raymond
Hartley Karen Hartley Paul Harvey David Haswell Ian Karl Haswell Victoria Hauxwell Richard
Havenhand Terence Hawkins Rodney Hawksfield David Hay Antony Hayes Mark Haywood
Barry Leslie Haywood Jeffrey Heatley Alan John Hedley Frederick Hedley Stephen Heeley
Gwyneth Heeley Roger Hemingway Lance Henderson Douglas Henderson Robert Henderson
John Henderson Peter Henderson Gordon Henderson Lynne Henderson Keith Hendley Philip
Hendry Patrick Henzell Alan Hepple Kevin Herbert George Herdman Andrew Hermeston
John Herring William Herron James Heslop David Heslop John Hetherington Paul Hewitson
Peter Hewitt Susan Hibbert Philip Hicklin Keith Higgins Maureen Higgins Michael Hildreth
Barry Hill Stephen Hill Richard Hill Christopher Hillaby Paul Hilton Colin Hilton Jeremy
Hindhaugh Karl Hindmarch John Hirst Laurence Hobson Philip Hodgkinson Ronald
Hodgkinson Peter Hodgson Thomas Hodgson David Hoey John Hogg Robert Hogg John Holder
Barry Holland Stephen Holland Scott Holliday Giles Hollinshead Keith Holmes John Hood Alan
Hope Robert Hopkins Paul Hopkinson Edward Hopkinson David Horn Kenneth Horn Ian
Horton Richard Houghton Raymond Hourigan Thomas Howard Ashley Howarth John Howe

Peter Howe Keith Howe Gail Howe Stephen Hownam Edward Hudson Peter Hudson Russell Hudson Peter Huggins John Hughes Raymond Hughes Robert Hughes John David Hughes-Lawson Ian Hugill Anthony Human Benjamin Humble David Humble Paul Humphrey Stephen Hunnam George Hunter Ian Thomas Hunter William Hunter Paul Hunter Jimmy Hunter Christopher Huntley Bryan Huntley Raymond Huntley Steven Hunton John Hurlbutt Peter Hurst Graeme Hurst Alan Hutchinson Thomas Hutchinson Ian Hutton George Hutton Leonard **I** Ion Trevor Irwin Richard Irwin David Irwing George Iveson Peter **J** Jackman Mary Jackman Walter Jackson Thomas Jackson Eric Jackson Keith Jackson Stephen Jackson Adrian Jackson Graeme Jackson Anthony Jackson Christopher Jacobson Kyle Jacobson Jason James John James Arthur James Keith James Lee Janagal Balras Jeffers David Jefferson David Jeffrey John Jeffrey Anthony Jeffrey Colin Jeffrey Colin Jennings Terence Jennings Peter Jerrome Philip Jobling Jeffery Jobling David Jobling George Jobling Darren Jobson Andrew Johnson Roger Johnson Ernest Johnson Robert Johnson Steward Johnson Richard Johnson John Johnson Charles Johnson Leslie Johnson Suzanne Johnson Ian Johnson David Johnson Mark Johnson Simon Johnston Paul Johnstone Peter Jones Alan Jones Darren Jones Robert Jones Glynn Jones Colin Jones Susan Jones Paul Jones Elizabeth Jordan Jordan Roy Joyce George **K** Kain Stephen Kane Terence Katsikis Costa C Kayll Leonard Keeler Kevin Keillor-White Melinda Keillor-White Melinda Keith Colin Kelly David Kelly Glyn Kelly Alan Kelly Andrew Kelly Christopher Kelly David Kennedy Allan Kennedy David Kennedy Christine Kennedy Christopher Kerr John Kerr Michael Kerr Ian Kershaw James Kew Kevin Kewbank Andrew Khatib Billy Kiernan Denis Kindred Keith King Anthony King Michael King Russell Kinniburgh Andrew Kipling Philip Kirby Darren Kirby Richard Kirk Stephen Kirkham Colin Kirkpatrick Colin Kirsopp George Kirsopp Andrew Kirsopp Simon Knight Edmund Knighton John **L** Laidler Stephen Laidler David Laidler Kevin Laight Jon Lamb Stephen Lambie Gary Lane Peter Lane Christopher Lane Andrew Lane Christopher Langley Rodney Langton William Lannighan Keith Larkin Christopher Latimer David Latimer Carl Lauder Tom Lavender Paul Laverick Henry Laverick Karl Laverty Paul Lavery William Lawrance Martin Lawrence William Laws John Laws William Lawson Debra Lawson Scott Lawton Kevin Laycock Timothy Leach David Lee Kevin Lee David Lee Michael Lee Anthony Legg Steven Legg Mark Leslie John Leslie Graeme Levee Arthur Lewis George Lewis Gordon Lewis David Liddle Michael Lilley Stephen Lillford John Lillford Andrew Lincoln James Lindley Ian Lineham Andrew Lineham Andrew Linsley David Linton Derek Linton Mark Liston David Little Barry Lively Martin Lively Martin Llewellyn Lee Lloyd Adrian Loader Colin Lock Ben Locke Robert Lockyear Arthur Loftus Brian Logan George Logan Julia Logan Lee Longmore Ian Longstaff John Longstaff Michael Lord Kevin Lorriman Derek Louis John Louth Peter Lovegrove William Lowe Arthur Lowery Richard Lowes Gary Lowes Andrew Lowson John Lowther Leonard Lowther Christopher Lugg Gary Luke Stephen Lumsdon Scott Lumsdon Kevin Lyall Thomas Lye Mark Lynass Stephen Lynass Stephen Lynch William Lynn Paul **M** Macdonald Colin Macdonald John Macfarlane Iain Macgregor Duncan Macintosh Tony Mackey David Macleod Hugh Maddison Stephen Maddox George Magnay Paul Mahan Bruce Mains Ronald Mair Carolyn Mair John Major George Makin Shaun Malley Steven Manderson Paul Mangan Michael Manson Kevin Manson Helen March Gerard Markwell Kenneth Markwell Anthony Markwick Paul Marley Kevin Marriott William Marriott Alan Marshall Thomas Marshall Glyn Marshall Kevin Marshall Keith Marshall Sean Marshall Brian Marshall Paul Marshall Barry Marshall Paul Mart Malcolm Martin Neville Martin Paul Martin David Martindale Alan Mason Godfrey Mason Frederick Mason Harold Mason Alan Mason David Mather Paul Mather Lance Matheson Alexander Matthews Keith Matthews Stuart Maugham Barry Maughan Alan May Stuart Mcaneny Don Mcardle Timothy Mccabe James Mccabe Christopher Mccallan Michael Mccallan Michael Mccarthy Trevor Mccoll John Mcconnell

William Mcconnell Martin Mcconville John Mccourt Peter Mccowliff John Mccoy Peter Mcdine Keith Mcdonald Jamie McDougall Callum Mcevoy Paul Mcewan Douglas Mcewen Peter Mcfarquhar Alan Mcginley Peter Mcgrath Stephen Mcgreevy Paul Mcgregor Bryan Mcguinness Malcolm Mcguinness Christopher Mcguire Colin Mcguire Colin Mckane James Mckay Keith Mckee Sean Mckenna Stephen Mckenzie Michael Mckie James Mckinnes Iain Mckitten Michael Mclachlan Ian Mclachlan John Mclaren Thomas Mclean Donald Mclean Richard Mcleod David Mcmahon Paul Mcmahon Keenan Mcmanus Patrick Mcmaster Paul Mcmeiken David Mcmeiken Ian Mcmillan John McMillan Brendan Mcmullen John Mcmullen George Mcmullon Alison Mcmurrough Ronald Mcnamara Robert Mcneil Stuart Mcnestry Joseph Mcnestry John Mcnestry Joseph Mcnestry John Mcpike Paul Mcquade John Mcqueen Richard Mcsherry Barry Mcskelly John Mcvey David Mead Darren Meadows Stephen Medhurst Lee Meisuria Gavin Melia Thomas Mellefont Thomas Melling James Mellish Paul Melrose Stewart Mennim Ian Meston Raymond Metcalf John Metcalf Gordon Metters Paul Middleton Sara Milburn Mervyn Milburn Norman Milburn Stephen Miller Stanley Miller George Miller John Miller Arthur Miller Garry Miller James Millican Kenneth Milne James Milton Alan Minikin William Mitchell Colin Mitchell David Mitchelson Robert Moat Pamela Mole Philip Monaghan Ronald Montague Reginald Montgomery Joseph Montgomery Kevin Moon Alfred Moor Trevor Moore Kenneth Moore Edward Moore Ian Moore Kenneth Moore Kevin Moore Christopher Moralee George Moran Richard Moran Neil Mordecai Lawrence Morgan Joseph Morgan Robert Morgan David Morland Philip Morley Christopher Morrell Derek Morrell Ronald Morrell Paul Morris Christopher Morrison Kenneth Mortimer Stanley Moses Thomas Moston Nicole Mowat George Mudie Peter Mulholland Robert Mulholland Reuben Mullarkey Michael Mullen George Mullen Benjamin Mulvaney John Murley Paul Murphy Dennis Murphy Stephanie Murphy Jeffrey Murray Michael Murray John Mustafa Bahri Mustard Lindsey Myers Paul N Naylor Keith Neasham Charles Neasham Stuart Nelson Robert Nelson Peter Nelson Garry Nelson Andrew Ness Janine Newman Pamela Newman David Newton Gary Newton Derick Newton Peter Nichol Colin Nicholls Robert Nichols John Nicholson Robert Nicholson James Nicholson Peter Nicholson Colin Nicholson Terence Nicholson Graeme Nicol Anthony Nielsen Michael Nixon Peter Nixon Gordon Noble Graham Noble Eric Noble Richard Noble Andrew Norman Edwin Norris David Nugent Steven O O'Boyle Ian O'Boyle Ian O'Brien Raymond O'Brien Keith O'Callaghan John O'Donnell Barry O'Donnell Terence O'Donnell Brian O'Donnell Derek O'Donnell Dennis O'Donnell Anthony O'Dwyer Brian Ogden Glenjames Ogden Stuart Roy O'Grady James O'Grady Shirley Oguona Daryl O'Kane Brendan O'Kane Anthony Okeefe Peter Oliver Brian Oliver John Oliver John Oliver Gary Oliver Edward Oliver John Olsen Grahame Olsen Grahame Olsson David Oman Michael O'Neill James O'Neill Vincent Ord Jeffrey Ord John Ord Dirk Orr James Orr David Osborn Natalie Osborne John Ould Peter Owen David Oxley Timothy P Padget Robert Page Ronald Palmer Frederick Panton Ian Parker Ronald Parkin Allan Parkinson William Parkinson Brian Parkinson Brian Parkinson David Parnaby David Parnaby Keith Pashley Adam Patrick Craig Patterson Susan Patterson Alan Patterson Bruce Pattison Arthur Pattison Dean Pattison Nicola Payn David Payne Brian Peacock Colin Pearce Keith Pearson Charles Pearson James Pearson Christopher Peck Brian Peel Steven Penman Richard Percy Alan Percy John Percy Richard Perkins Arthur Perry Anthony Perry Mark Peters Gordon Peters Gerald Petford James Petre George Phelan Raymond Phelan Susan Phelan Mark Phillips Stanley Phillips David Phillipson George Phillipson Keith Pickett Colin Pinder Keith Pinder Stuart Pinkerton Alexander Pinkerton Norman Pinkney Graham Plant John Pollock Stephen Poole William Poppett Kevan Poppett Ian Porteous Cameron Porter David Porter Ronald Porterfield John Potter Robinson Potter George Potts James Potts Philip Powell Keith Powell Robert Powell Barry Powell Colin Pratt Roger Pratt John Prentice Simon Price Edwin

Price Raymond   Price John Priest Raymond   Pringle Kenneth Pringle Stephen Pringle John
Pritchard Susan Proctor Brian Proctor Lee Proud Jonathan Prudham Frederick Prudham Steven
Pude Joseph Purves David Purvis David **Q** Quigley Paul Quinan Leslie Quinn Michael Quinn
Gary Race Sydney **R** Race Alan   Rae John   Railton Andrew   Raine Dennis Ramm Graeme
Ramsay Duncan Ramsay Ian Ramshaw Marshall Ramshaw David Rand Wayne Raper Anthony
Rawlings Keith Ray Terence   Rayne Keith Rayner Derek Reah George   Reah Richard   Reah
Christian Reay John   Redfearn Michael   Reed Matthew Reid Michael Renfree John Rennie Gordon
Renton Peter   Reynolds Keith Reynolds Alfred   Reynolds Heidi   Richards Brian   Richards James
Richardson David Richardson John   Richardson Ian   Richardson Ian Richardson Karen
Richardson Allyn Richardson Raymond Richardson Thomas   Richardson Allan Richardson Gary
Richardson Thomas Richley George Rickaby Richard   Rickerby John   Riddell Charles   Ridley John
Ridley Stuart   Riley Paul   Ritchie Marshall   Ritson Clifford Ritson Michael   Robb Graham   Robbie
Brian Roberts Joseph   Roberts Jonathon   Roberts Matthew   Robertson Paul   Robertson Ian
Robertson Stuart   Robertson Jim Robinson John Robinson David   Robinson Wayne Robinson
Michael Robinson Alan Robinson Jeffrey Robinson Kenneth Robinson Marcus Robinson Keith
Robinson Ronald Robinson Peter Robinson Iain Robinson Neil Robinson Ian Robinson Marcus
Robinson Simon Robinson Adam Robinson Peter Robson Derek Robson John   Robson Brian
Robson Eric Robson David Robson Colin Robson Stuart Robson Melvyn Robson Sharon Robson
Alan Robson Stephen Robson Paul   Robson Keith Robson Nigel   Robson Alan Robson Karl
Robson David   Roche Paul Pa Rochester Stephen Rochester David   Rochford Anthony Roddy
Bernard   Rodgerson Robert Roffe John   Rosby Christopher   Rose David   Ross Barry Ross Alan
Routledge Eric Rowe Ronald   Rowe Robert   Rowe Ronald   Rowell Alan   Rowell Peter Rowell
Mark Rowland David   Rowley David Royal David   Royal Christopher Royal William   Rucroft
Kevin Rudd Melvin   Rumney John   Russell Paul   Rutherford Iain   Ryan Glenn **S** Sabbatinelli
Nicholas Sabiston James Sabiston Jeffery Salters Paul Sample Niall Sanderson James Sanderson
George Sanderson David   Sanderson David Sanson Phillip   Sargeant John   Sargeant Lee   Sargent
Adrian Sarin Neil Scales Alan Scarr William Scorer William   Scorer Gary Scott Robert Scott John
Scott Jacqueline Scott Peter   Scott William   Scott Paul Scott Martin Scrimshaw Lesley Scrimshaw
Christopher Seddon David   Selby Luke Selby Terence Semple John Semple Stephen Seth Russell
Seth Yvonne Sewell John   Sewell Stephen Sharkey David   Sharp Thomas Sharpe Kenneth Shaw
Brian Shaw Martin   Shayshutt Colin Shepherd Gerald Shepherd Jay   Shiel David Shiel Graham
Shippen Geoffrey   Short Leslie Shorting Beverly Jane Shorting Beverley   Shrubb Paul   Shrubb
Geoffrey   Shrubb Mark   Sidaway Thomas   Simpson David   Simpson Derek Simpson David
Simpson Jeffrey Simpson David   Simpson Kevin Simpson David Simpson Paul   Sirey Kevin
Skelton John   Skelton Mark   Skinner William   Skivington Arthur   Slack Martin Slater Ian Sloan
Scott Sloanes John   Smailes Gary   Smallwood William   Smart Graeme   Smeltzer Neil Smiles
Adrian   Smiles Steven   Smith Alan   Smith Andrew   Smith Gordon Smith Neil   Smith Joseph
Smith Kenneth Smith Derek Smith George   Smith David Smith James Smith Charles Smith Peter
Smith Jane   Smith David Smith Paul   Smith Leonard   Smith Gordon Smith Neil Smith Graham
Smith Gary   Smith Trevor Smith Trevor   Smith David   Smith Stephen   Smith Stephen Smith Sean
Smith Andrew   Smith Derek Smith Gary Smith Jonathan   Smith Andrew   Smith Ross   Smith
David   Snaith Michael Snelling Tammey Marie Snowdon Darren Soady Karen   Soden Kenneth
Soulsby Leslie Soulsby Paul South Terence Southern Rachel Southern Philip   Sowerby Philip
Spence Marshall   Spence George   Spencer Steven Spencer Scott Spendiff Malcolm Spink William
Spires Edward   Spoors David   Sproat John   Spruce David   Stabler David Stabler Pauline Stafford
William   Stagg Douglas   Stainton Peter Standish John   Standish John   Stanger Derek   Stanley
Lawrence   Stanton Graham Steele Anthony   Steele Penelope   Steele Robert   Steinberg Derek
Stephens David   Stephens David   Stephenson John   Stephenson John   Stephenson David

Stephenson John Stephenson Jeffrey Stephenson Norman Stevenson Raymond Stewart Keith Stewart Kenneth Stewart Kevin Stewart William Stewart Ian John Stewart Christopher Stirland Matthew Stockley Brian Stokoe Stephen Stone David Stone Christopher Stowell Stratton Peter Straughan Alan Stringer Christopher Stronach Peter Stuart Brian Stubbings James Stubbs John Stubbs Gary Sturrock Trevor Stuthridge Martin Summerell Trevor Summerly Gary Summers David Summerside George Sweeney Kevin Syrett James |T| Tague Trevor Tait Melvyn Tait Alexander Tait Paul Tarbett David Tate Ian Tate Mark Taviner David Taylor James Taylor Alan Taylor Stanley Taylor Laurence Taylor George Taylor Thomas Taylor Kim Taylor Thomas Taylor Robert Taylor Stephen Taylor James Taylor Ian Taylor Gavin Teasdale Garry Telfer Robert Telford David Templeton Barrie Templey Robert Tennick Christopher Thain Norman Theisinger Craig Thew Lee Thielman William Thomas Steven Thompson Reginald Thompson Jeffrey Thompson John Thompson James Thompson Noel Thompson Brian Thompson David Thompson Stuart Thompson Michael Thompson John Thompson James Thompson Laurence Thompson Paul Thompson Colin Thompson Neil Thompson Graeme Thompson Richard Thompson Steven Thompson Leslie Thompson Michael   Thompson Greg Thomson Shaun Thornby John Thurgood Alan Tibbs Michael Tiernan David Tiffin George Tiffin Guy Tinnion Brian Tiplady Robert Tiplady Joseph Tippins William Tippins Brian Todd Kenneth Tough Richard Tough Leslie Towers Paul Trafford Andrew Trainer Brian Trainor Nicholas Treleaven Christopher Trenfield Gregory Trenfield Lloyd Trevithick Peter Trodden Stephen Trotter Alan Truman David Tubbrit Chris Tucker Colin Tulip John Tulip Craig Tully Bernard Turnbull Ian Turnbull Brian Turnbull Neil Turnbull Paul Turnbull James Turnbull Jeffrey Turner Jimmy Turner Collin Turner David Turner Harry Turpin David Turrell James |U| Urwin Alan Urwin Robert Usher Jeffrey Usher Edward Usher Alan Usher Kevin Usher Christopher Usher Christopher Usher Adrian |V| Van-Enk Peter Van-Enk Fiona Vasey John David Vaughan Thomas Veitch Peter Veitch Thomas Venters Michael Venus Ronald Venus William Vickers Michael Vickery Simon Vinton William |W| Waddell Philip Wake John Walkden Stephen Walker Ian Walker James Walker Beverley Walker Ian Walker Alan Walker Dean Walker Stephen Walker Benjamin Walker Brad Walker Steven Wallace Raymond Wallace Scott Wallace Jon Wallbank Gary Walls Michael Walmsley David Walsh John Walsh Ian Walters Keith Walton Robert Walton Alan Walton Dale Walton David Wanless Robert Warbrick Ian Ward Bruce Ward David Ward Martin Ward Vincent Ward Carolyn Warden Christopher Wardingham Shaun Warne Ian Garry Warren Mark Waters Norman Watson David Watson David Watson Philip Watson Paul Watt David Waugh Brian Waugh Brian Wayman Stephen Weatherstone Anthony Weatherstone Anthony Webb Eric Webb Terence Webb Duncan Websdale Charles Webster John Weddle Edward Weddle John Weighill Peter Welford Michael Welsh John West William Westgarth Mark Westgarth Mark Whellans Gillian White Alan White Kevinjames White Christopher White Ivan Paul White John White John Whiteman Brian Whiteman Alan Whitfield Steven Whitfield Colin Whitfield Graham Whitfield Edward Whitfield John Whitley Martyn Wilcox Peter Wilcox Stephen Wildhirt Stanley Wilkes Ian Wilkinson Brian Wilkinson Henry Wilkinson Barry Wilkinson Martin Wilkinson Jeffrey Wilkinson Kenneth Wilkinson Kristian Williams Timothy Williams Kevin Williams Steven Williams Jonathan Williams Kevan Williamson Norman Williamson Derek Williamson Darren Willis Colin Willis Christopher Willis Mark Wilson Alan Wilson Roy Wilson Derek Wilson Brian Wilson John Wilson Eric Wilson David Wilson Stephen Wilson Garry Wilson Brian Wilson Julie Wilson Kenneth Wilson Adrian Wilson Stephen Wilson Peter Wilson Graeme Wilson Stephen Wilson Michael Wiltshire Anthony Wind Anthea Winter John Witherspoon Mark Withycombe David Witty Philip Wood Andrew Wood Anthony Wood Michael Wood Ian Woodhouse Paul Woods Alan Woof Brian Worthington George Wrathmall Keith Wright Brian Wright Peter Wright George Wright Philip Wright Robert Wright Mark Wyatt

David Yates Gary <u>Y</u> Yates Brian Youll Ian Young Roy Young David Young Barry Young Geoffrey Young Thomas Young Michael Young Steven Young John Young Neil Young Lloyd Young Malcolm Young Paul Younger Graeme Younger Norman Yoxall John

Above: **Fire Brigade Long Service & Good Conduct Medal.**

Presented on completion of 20 years service.

Under the terms of a Royal Warrant instituted on 1st June 1954 in which Her Majesty the Queen made provision for honouring long and meritorious service. The award is only made to those who have twenty years unbroken service and have proved themselves to be of impeccable character.

Above: **Saint Florian.** Patron Saint of Firefighters Worldwide.

127

About the Author

Dave Walmsley BA(Hons) CertEd(FE) GIFireE RAFVR(T)

Dave Walmsley served in the Tyne & Wear Fire & Rescue Service for 33 years. He joined as a bright eyed 19 year old Fireman at VICTOR (Gateshead) in 1974. He retired as a philosophical Station Officer (Watch Manager) from Sunderland Legislative Fire Safety Department (now Protection & Technical).

In between was a varied and well travelled career throughout the Brigade. He also served at, MIKE (Fulwell), ROMEO (Tunstall), YANKEE (Swalwell), BHQ – DELTA (Newcastle), BTC Brigade Training Centre (Washington), NOVEMBER (Sunderland Central) & JULIET (Tynemouth) LFS. Including various temporary positions and detachments it's safe to say he visited every station within the Brigade.

A Graduate of the IFE – (Institution of Fire Engineers) he holds a BA(Hons) in Education, CertEd(FE), NEBOSH and IOSH. He is a serving officer (Flight Lieutenant) in the RAFVR(T) -Royal Air Force Volunteer Reserve (Training) branch. A holder of the Fire Brigade Long Service & Good Conduct Medal, (20 years) 30 years Certificate and the Queen's Golden Jubilee Medal.

He is a founder member of the Washington History Society and Northern Writers Group.